THIS JO

BELONGS TO

....

Happy Easter

Copyright © 2019 by Jungle Sprout

FIRST EDITION

Why did the egg cross the internet?

To get to the other site.

What game does the Easter Bunny like to play on his driveway?

Hopscotch.

What does the Easter Bunny use to keep his fur so neat?

He uses a hare brush.

What do you say to the
Easter Bunny on his birthday?

Hoppy birthday!

What does the Easter Bunny
plant next to the green beans
in his garden?

Jelly beans.

How was the chicken able
to get home from work so
fast?

It used the eggs-press
lane.

What's the best game to play on Easter?

Basket ball.

How do you make an egg roll?

Push it down a hill.

Knock Knock
Who's there?
Carrie
Carrie who?

Carrie my Easter basket please, it's too heavy.

Why do chickens lay eggs?

If they drop the eggs, they'll break.

Why did the Easter Bunny cross the road?

To get the chicken's eggs.

Knock Knock
Who's there?
Felix
Felix who?
Felix-cited about Easter!

What do you get when you cross the Easter Bunny with Kermit the Frog?

A bunny ribbit.

Which US city has 9 million eggs living in it?

New Yolk City.

Why wouldn't the Easter Bunny cross the road?

Because he's not a chicken.

What looks like half an Easter Bunny?

The other half!

Why did the Easter Bunny throw the clock out the window?

He wanted to see time fly.

How does the Easter Bunny travel on vacation?

On hare planes.

What do you get when you cross a hen with a cement truck?

A brick layer.

How do young chickens dance to slow songs?

Chick-to-chick.

What you get if when cross the Easter Bunny with Ant Man?

Bugs Bunny.

What do you call a rabbit comedian?

A funny bunny.

What happened after the Easter Bunny got married?

They lived hoppily ever after.

How do you know when the Easter Bunny likes a book?

Because he'll tell you it's egg-cellent.

Where did the Easter Bunny go for a new tail?

To a retail store.

What did the egg say to the clown?

You crack me up.

Knock, knock.
Who's there?
Harvey.
Harvey who?
Harvey happy Easter.

Why did the lamb call the police?

He had been fleeced

What do you call a dancing lamb?

A baa-lerina!

What makes the Easter Bunny so lucky?

He always has four rabbits feet on him!

What did the Spanish egg farmer say to his hens every night?

Oh lay.

What is the fastest way to send a postcard to the Easter Bunny?

Using hare mail.

What do you get if you cross Winnie the Pooh and the Easter Bunny?

A honey bunny.

What do you call a chicken in a shellsuit?

An egg!

What do you call a lamb with no legs?

A cloud.

Where did the lamb get a haircut?

The baa-baa shop!

What did the Easter Bunny put a dictionary in his pants?

He wanted to be a smarty pants.

How does the Easter Bunny's day always end?

With a Y.

Knock Knock
Who's there?
Hans.
Hans who?

Hans off my Easter eggs buster!

How does the Easter Bunny keep his fur from getting messed up?

He uses lots of hare spray.

Where do lambs take a bath?

In a baaaa-th tub!

What did one Easter egg say to the other Easter egg?

Want to hear a funny yolk?

What happens when you
tickle an egg?

It cracks up.

How does the Easter
Bunny stay in such good
shape?

Egg-xercise.

What did the Easter
Bunny do after it's
wedding?

Went on a nice
bunnymoon.

What did they call the Easter Bunny after he aced the math test?

A hare-brain.

~~~~~~~~

What did the lamb want to do?

To wool the world.

~~~~~~~~

Knock Knock
Who's there?
Hominy.
Hominy who?
Hominy Easter eggs did you find?

Where did the Easter Bunny learn how to ski?

The bunny hill.

How does the Easter Bunny know where he burried treasure?

Eggs marks the spot.

Knock Knock
Who's there?
Tommy.
Tommy who?
Tommy aches from eating too much Easter Chocolate

What does the Easter Bunny do when he gets out of the shower?

Uses a hare dryer.

What do you call a scrambled egg wearing a cowboy hat?

A western omelette.

Knock, knock.
Who's there?
Sherwood.
Sherwood who?
Sherwood like to have a chocolate Easter bunny.

What can you call the Easter Bunny when he has the sniffles?

A runny bunny.

What do you call the Easter Bunny the day after Easter?

Eggshausted!

What do you get when you cross Dumbo the elephant with the Easter Bunny?

An elephant who always remember to eat all of his carrots.

Why did the egg cross the road?

To get to the shell station.

Why shouldn't you tease a egg white?

They can't take a yolk.

Where do lambs go on vacation?

To the baaaaaahamas.

What kind of jewelry does the Easter Bunny wear?

A 14 carrot gold necklace.

How does a rabbit throw a tantrum?

He gets hopping mad.

What stories does the Easter Bunny like best?

The ones with hoppy endings!

What do you call a egg prankster?

A practical yolker.

Why couldn't the little lamb play outside?

It was being baaaaaaaad!

Knock Knock
Who's there?
Harris.
Harris who?
Harris another word for bunny!

What did one colored egg say to the other?

'Heard any good yolks lately!'

What do you need if your chocolate eggs mysteriously disappear?

You need an eggsplanation!

Why did the bunny go to the dance?

To do the bunny hop!

What do eggs do for fun at parties?

Sing kari-yolkie.

How does Easter end?

With an R!

What did the grey rabbit say to the blue rabbit?

Cheer up!

Did you about the Easter Bunny that sat on an ice-cream cone?

It's a long cold tail!

What do you call an Easter egg you have dropped on the floor?

Crackers!

Do you know how the Easter bunny stays in shape?

Hareobics.

Why are you stuffing all that Easter candy into your mouth?

Because it doesn't taste as good if I stuff it in my ears.

What do you call an egg who travels around the world?

An eggs-plorer.

How do you catch a rabbit?

Make a noise like a carrot.

What did the egg learn about being part of an omelet?

It found out it wasn't all it was cracked up to be.

What did the Easter Bunny say to the carrot who was moving away?

Been nice gnawing you.

Why did the Easter Bunny eat the gold ring?

He was told it was 18 carrots.

What kind of bunny can't hop?

A chocolate one!

What kind of eggs live by the sea?

Egg shells.

How many eggs can you eat on an empty stomach?

One. After that, your stomach won't be empty anymore.

Who tells the best
egg jokes?

Comedi-hens.

What do you get when
you cross a chicken with
an alien?

E.T. the
eggs-traterrestrial.

Why was the Easter
Bunny so upset when he
looked in the mirror?

He was having a bad
hare day.

Why didn't the bunny hop?

No bunny knows.

Why do rabbits eat carrots?

Because they don't want to be nearsighted!

How does the Easter Bunny paint all the Easter eggs?

He hires Santa's elves during the off season.

How can you tell the Easter Bunny was a boyscout?

He helps little old bunnies cross the street.

How do ghosts order their eggs?

Terri-fried.

What do you call a lamb covered in chocolate?

A Candy Baa.

What's yellow, has long ears, and grows on trees?

The Easter Bunana!

How do you make a rabbit stew?

Make it wait for three hours!

How did the egg get up the hill?

It scrambled up.

What kind of car does the Easter Bunny drive?

A hop rod.

Which side of the Easter Bunny has the most fur?

The outside.

Why can't the Easter Bunny's ear be twelve inches long?

Because then it would be a foot.

Which part did the egg get in the TV show?

He was cast as an egg-stra

How do eggs get off a highway?

By using the eggs-it.

Knock Knock
Who's there?
Berlin.
Berlin who?
Berlin the water for hard-boiled Easter eggs.

What kind of car does a sheep like to drive?

A Lamborghini

What was the egg's favorite tree?

A y-oak tree.

How do rabbits stay cool during the summer?

With hare conditioning.

Where do eggs go to college?

Yokelahomia State.

What track event to chickens compete in?

Relay race.

Knock, knock.
Who's there?
Chuck.
Chuck who?
Chuckolate Easter bunnies are my favorite.

What kind of car does the Easter Bunny drive?

A hop rod.

Which side of the Easter Bunny has the most fur?

The outside.

Why can't the Easter Bunny's ear be twelve inches long?

Because then it would be a foot.

What do chickens serve at their Easter parties?

Coop cakes.

Where can you find the most information about eggs?

In the hencyclopedia.

What's hard to beat in the morning?

A boiled egg.

Where can you get ice cream for Easter?

Basket Robbins

How can you tell when a chicken doesn't get your joke?

By the eggspression on it's face.

Which bedtime stories does the Easter Bunny like most?

Hairy tales with hoppy endings.

What did the person say when the egg said hello?

Ahhhhhh – a talking egg..

What do you call a pig who wakes up with a rash?

Ham and Eggzema.

How did the egg get out of the sticky situation?

Non-stick spray.

How do rabbits stay cool during the summer?

With hare conditioning.

What do chicken families do on nice afternoons?

They go on peck-nics.

Knock Knock
Who's there?
Carrie
Carrie who?
Carrie my Easter basket please, it's too heavy

Why did the chicken go for a walk?

She needed the Egg-ercise.

Since fruit comes from fruit trees, where do chickens come from?

A poul-tree.

Why was the chef called a bully?

He beat the eggs.

Why did the Easter bunny shave off his fur?

Global warming!

Why is Easter like whipped cream and a cherry?

Because it's always on a sundae!

How many Easter eggs can you put in an empty basket?

Only one – after that it's not empty any more!

What do chickens call a test at school?

An eggs-amination.

Why did the egg go to school?

To get an egg-u-cation.

Knock, Knock.
Who's there?
Omelette.
Omelette who?
Omelette smarter than you think.

What do you call a bunny with a large brain?

An egghead.

Where does Valentine's Day comes after Easter?

In the dictionary.

What did the egg quarterback do when it saw the frying pan coming his way?

It scrambled.

Why was the Easter rabbit rubbing his head?

Because he had a eggache!

How did the fritata find out it was sick?

A doctor eggs-amined it.

Knock knock.
Who's there?
Chicken.
Chicken who?
Chicken your pockets, maybe you'll find it.

What did Snow White name her pet chicken?

Egg white.

What's the worst crime in the egg law book?

Poaching.

What style of music does the Easter Bunny's like to listen to?

Hip Hop.

What do you end up when a
hen lays it's egg on a roof?

An eggroll.

What do you call an egg who
can't stay awake?

Egg-zosted.

Why is the bunny the
luckiest animal?

Because they have
four rabbits feet!

What do you call the Easter Bunny when he has fleas?

Bugs Bunny.

What did the bunny want to do when he grew up?

Join the Hare Force.

What do you get if you pour hot water down a rabbit hole?

Hot cross bunnies.

What do you get when you cross a chicken and the Easter Bunny?

A good Easter.

Why does the Easter Bunny have a shiny nose?

Because the powder puff is on the other end!

Why did a fellow rabbit say that the Easter Bunny was self-centered?

Because he is eggocentric.

Who delivers Easter treats to all the fish in the sea?

The Oyster Bunny!

What did the momma egg say to her baby egg?

You're egg-stra special.

Knock, Knock?
Who's there?
Ann.
Ann who?
Ann-other Easter Bunny.

What do you call 13 rabbits marching backwards?

A receding hareline.

What do chickens say to get across a crowded barn?

Eggs-cuse me.

How many eggs does it take to screw in a light bulb?

None, silly! Eggs don't have hands.

Where does the Easter Bunny get all of the eggs he hides?

He gets them from an eggplant.

What proof is there that carrots are good for the eyes?

You never see rabbits wearing eye glasses.

Knock Knock
Who's there?
Handsome.
Handsome who?

Handsome Easter candy to me please.

What does Frosty the Snowman say every time he comes to life again on Easter?

Hoppy Birthday!

Where do chickens live on the west coast?

SandiEGGo.

Who wrote the books "Great Eggspectations" and "Hard-Boiled Times?"

Charles Chickens.

How do you get inside a chicken barn?

Use the hen-trance.

Where does the Easter bunny eat breakfast?

IHOP!

What did the chicken order at Starbucks?

An Eggspreso.

Made in the USA
San Bernardino, CA
02 April 2020